FOOTPRINTS ON MY HEART

A Journey of Living Life After Losing My Baby

Julie Linck

Copyright © 2019 by Julie Linck

All rights reserved. No part of this book may be reproduced or used in any manner without written permission of the publisher or the copyright owner/ author except under Fair Use provisions of the U.S. Copyright law.

Contents

Introduction 5

Chapter 1: Mia's Story 6

Chapter 2: The Grief Journey 13

Chapter 3: Get Connected 15

Chapter 4: Significant Days 17

Chapter 5: Returning to Work 18

Chapter 6: Sharing With Others 19

Chapter 7: Sibling Grief 21

Chapter 8: Holiday Grief 25

Chapter 9: Father's Grief 28

Chapter 10: Mother's Grief 31

Chapter 11: Honor Their Memories 35

Chapter 12: Pictures are Priceless 37

Chapter 13: Journal the Journey 38

Chapter 14: A Chest Full of Hope 41

Chapter 15: Charms that bring Comfort 42

Chapter 16: Family Creations 43

Chapter 17: Foundations & Fundraisers 44

Chapter 18: Grow a Garden 45

Conclusion 46

Introduction

As parents, when we lose our children we grieve for the memories not made: those milestones that they'll never hit. We feel the loss but they're still a part of our family. So it is up to us to tell their story. As I look back and see the journey I've traveled these last 18 years, I see that I am further away from that pain that once kept me in bed; instead I've learned how to live with it. Some years I cry, and some I don't (although, there was a time I did think I wouldn't stop). However, I am so thankful to God for giving me Mia and making her a part of my story. Even though it is a heartbreaking and painful one, it's the story God wrote for my life. I choose to look for the positive things her life brings to mine, even all these years later. She's led me to a deeper faith in God, allowing me to be stronger and more brave in new situations and has given me the ability to help others who wear these similar shoes. It is my hope that whoever reads this will be able to help themselves, or someone they love, ease the burden of the journey ahead.

CHAPTER 1
Mia's Story

(Written December 12, 2001.... 3 days after her death)

The day we found out that we were having another baby we were in shock. We had just lost our dog, my mom was having heart surgery and our house was infested with termites. It was the furthest thing from our minds. Eric was only nine months old and I was scared of the idea of having two children so close together, but Tony literally within minutes of learning the news said, "We're great parents now, having two will make us even better parents." It was from that point on that I was so excited to be pregnant again. I even made the comment that Eric would have a little sister.

Mia's pregnancy was so different than Eric's. I felt great, didn't get sick, didn't gain the weight, wasn't as tired, carried her differently; all these things convinced me I was going to have a girl. Tony and I needed to decide if we wanted to know the sex of the baby. He wanted to be surprised, I wanted to know for one reason, so we could be more prepared. Our extra bedroom wasn't painted in girl colors and Eric's clothes were the wrong season; Tony finally agreed that it made sense to find out.

On August 1, 2001, we had the ultrasound - just three days after my birthday. We were told we were having a girl. I didn't even blink, I knew that was what we were going to be told. I left that office feeling so blessed and lucky that I was going to have one of each. Tony was just as excited, except he was more nervous handling "girl issues" after being around Eric for so long.

As Mia grew inside me I began to know her personality. She constantly kicked and moved. There were times she made my stomach look like a punching bag. Often times throughout the day my stomach would change shape. She was a mover and a shaker!

Eric began to realize that there was some sort of change. My belly was bigger and he thought it was funny to see my belly button popped out like a Thanksgiving turkey. When you asked him to kiss the baby, he'd lift my shirt and kiss my belly. Even as we started getting her room ready, he'd go in and play with all of the baby toys and wonder why they were in this room we never go in.

I had so much fun getting her room ready. My mom and dad had repainted the furniture. The furniture was my mom's when she was young, then was mine when I was little and now it was Mia's. I was looking forward to the little things like brushing her hair, dressing her up and experiencing all those things in a mother/daughter relationship.

I don't think I could have been more ready for another baby. We had the room ready, formula and diapers bought, car seat installed and bottles washed. All we needed was her home with us.

We went in on November 26, 2001 for what we thought was her arrival. I was contracting at school that day and as the afternoon and evening went on the contractions were getting closer. Tony and I did our walking pattern around the hospital to see if I would dilate anymore. I ended up being dilated between a 2 and a 3. After spending the night in the hospital for observation, the contractions disappeared and we went home.

I spent that week having contractions that were inconsistent and I spent the week just resting. On Sunday December 2, 2001 I woke up feeling lousy. I was more tired, kind of nauseous and as the day went on, I developed a headache that became unbearable. Early afternoon, Tony took my temperature and it was 102° and was continuing to climb. Tony and I went to the hospital where they admitted me and started to work on getting my fever down. I was held for observation that night and all day Monday.

Late Monday afternoon, I was still not feeling well and was told I would be staying. My fever would spike and go down, spike and go down. At 6:00 that evening I got a severe abdominal cramp that was not a contraction. My fever was up to 102.5° and I was in pain. My doctor said it was time to get the baby out.

At 7:00 pm my water broke and labor began. Shortly after 8:30 pm I was told that because of my fever, I couldn't have any drugs to help me with the pain. That was a scary moment. The pain became so intense that I could not take it. At 12:30 am I was dilated at a 6 and the nurse finally gave me Demerol which was to take the edge off. It didn't. All it did was calm me down enough between contractions - enough that 20 minutes later I was at a 10 and ready to push. They kept telling me not to push, but that wasn't possible. A resident doctor ended up coming to "catch" Mia as she made her way into this world. At 1:04 am on December 4, 2001 we had our beautiful baby girl, Mia Suzanne Linck.

Mia was checked over by NICU doctors because I was sick and after about an hour or so after delivery, I was sent to have a CAT scan to see what was wrong with me. Mia spent the night in the regular nursery. It was late morning when her temperature dropped and they moved her to the NICU to maintain her body temp. We were told that she

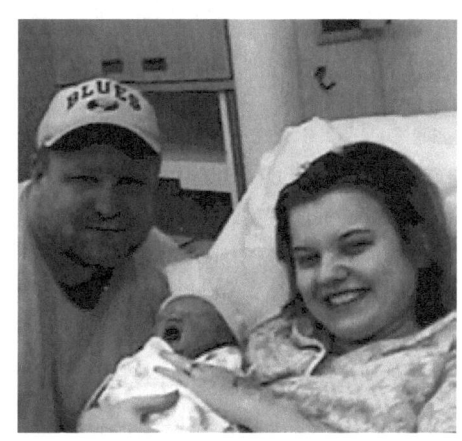

Chapter 1: Mia's Story | 7

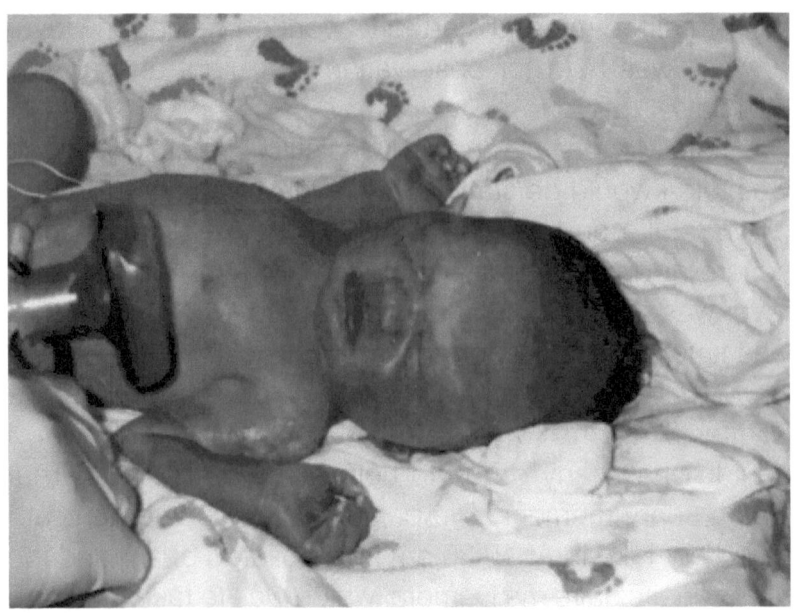

would be treated with antibiotics as a precautionary measure.

The hardest part was, with me not being fever free, I couldn't go see or hold my baby. I had to be fever free for 24 hours. We were counting down the minutes until 2:45 am on Wednesday. When the time rolled around, I could go and sit with her. She was still in the isolette, so I could only hold her during feeding times. I planned to go at 4:00 am to feed her.

At 3:45 am, right before I was to leave, my vitals were taken and my fever spiked to 100.6, meaning I couldn't go to feed or see Mia. I was devastated. Finally at 4:00 am on Thursday I got to hold my baby girl and feed her. I remember the feeling of joy holding her and seeing how beautiful she was.

I also remember feeling so thankful that she seemed to have the smallest problem in the NICU. We would be bringing her home in a matter of days, not months.

Friday morning at 5:00 am, the nurse practitioner woke me up to tell me that Mia's coloring was disconcerting and that she had developed a fever. They told me all the tests they were going to run to find the cause of the infection. Our pediatrician said it was overkill, but that they would find it.

Late Friday night, I was discharged and sent home. It was the hardest thing I had to do by leaving my baby at the hospital while I came home.

Saturday afternoon I went to feed Mia. I was so excited about her appearance and that her fever was going down. Even the nurse practitioner commented on how much better she looked. Tony and I came up later that evening to give her 10:00 pm feeding. She looked even better than the afternoon and her fever broke when we were there. We had gone home on cloud-nine feeling that everything was going to be ok.

Sunday morning we woke up and called to check on her. They had run an EKG on her heart because of an episode that caused her heart rate to increase to the 220's. Tony and I got there to find out we had to leave because they were putting an IV in her and taking her off all feedings. Her heart was showing signs of stress and they put her on oxygen and a bed warmer to her body didn't have to do any work. Tony and I couldn't even touch her. It was hard to watch her lie there and know we couldn't help or comfort her.

We went home quietly thinking of what we could do to help her. I know for me that this was the first time I was scared about her not making it. When we went home all we could do was think of her. I called to make sure that

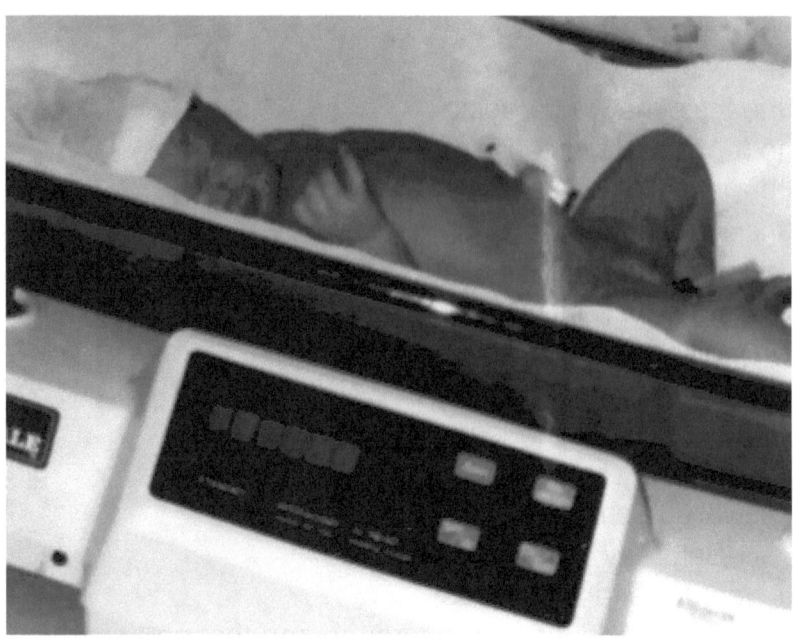

she was still the same (we were told it could get worse before it gets better) and we heard worse. Her platelet count was down and they had increased her oxygen. Eric had brought Tony his shoes, like it was a sign that he needed to go. So Tony left to be with her.

About an hour and a half later, the doctor called to explain that her oxygen levels had decreased and that she was now on a ventilator. He told me that her chances of beating this were far greater than not. I talked to Tony to let him know I was on my way up and he assured me it was not life threatening and things were looking better. Exactly one minute before my parents arrived to take me to the hospital, the nurse called to tell me she wasn't doing well and to bring the whole family.

I remember praying the whole way there and Eric had a look on him like he sensed that something was wrong. When I got there, her heart rate had fallen into the 60's and they were never able to get it back. There was nothing they could do. Tony and I had lost our beautiful baby girl. We didn't get it, we don't get it and we are still wondering; why us?

We had such big plans to bring her home and be a family. When Eric saw her for the first time he smiled from ear to ear. It broke our hearts to see how much love he had for her already and she didn't get to know him.

The only thing that we can come to terms with is that God needed an angel and she was it. We know that she has become our guardian as these past three days Tony and I have been more in sync with each other than ever. We are thinking and feeling the same way knowing that it's because of her we are growing closer together. Not everyone is lucky enough to meet his or her angel, but we were blessed by knowing her for the nine months she grew inside of me and her five days here on earth.

We will work through this and having each other and family and friends will make each day a little easier. We are fortunate to have Eric to help us and know that Mia touched so many lives in her short while with us. She had a purpose here and as each day goes by we will begin to understand what that was.

*After this was written, we learned through an autopsy, that Mia had a ½ inch hole in her heart along with meningitis. Doctors believe that the two together compromised her health and caused her to pass away.

CHAPTER 2

The Grief Journey

Grief is a rollercoaster of emotions and there is no set guide for how the ride will go. The thing about grief is that there is no "one way" to fix it and despite how we think we must feel, it's ok, not to feel ok. Your life has forever changed and you will have to learn how to figure out how to function as your best self in that new life.

As I began to figure out this new life for me, I had to travel with a share of setbacks along the journey. Two months after Mia passed away, when I had just returned to work, Eric, just 18 months old, was sick. He too was diagnosed with meningitis, which our doctor said was like lightning striking the same place twice. We spent another five days in the same hospital until the viral infection had run its course. I cried the entire way home because when I had left that hospital two months before I had left empty handed. I was so thankful that this time I had my child with me.

On December 9, 2002, I went into labor with my third child and second daughter, Molly Rene. This was the first anniversary of Mia's passing. Thankfully, the doctors were able to slow my labor enough to have her birth date the following day. But what were the odds that on Molly's first birthday she would be in the hospital being tested for meningitis? Luckily, she didn't have meningitis, but as you could imagine, this sent my anxiety through the roof. I would let my mind jump on the crazy train and always feared the worst. In my mind, a common cold would mean my children could lose their life. Through the years, I've battled with my share of panic and anxiety attacks trying to stay off the crazy train as best I could. However, through these struggles along the way, I've managed to find ways to incorporate Mia's memory into our family life and have found that as time passes, I've been able to adjust to this new normal.

CHAPTER 3

Get Connected

A common reaction after loss is to retract and isolate yourself from others and life happening around you. It's easier not to "deal" with people. You don't want to deal with your emotions, all of it together, can make it an easy trap to fall into. After Mia died, I didn't think I could function. I had so many "what ifs" that played in my mind and wondered what I could have done differently to protect her. I remember there were days just lying in bed while others took care of our 1 ½ year old son. One day, while flipping through a self-help book that was gifted to me, I came across a quote that said, "You can be bitter or you can be better." Those words struck a chord. I could be angry at the situation or angry at God for allowing others to have their babies, but instead took mine. I could keep lying in bed or I could get up and give my son the best version of myself. I didn't want to miss out on his childhood too. So, that was the day that I got up and took my first step towards living again. We got connected with a local support group, Share. We found ourselves meeting with other parents who were walking in our shoes. I remember meeting a mom who had lost her daughter 11 years before Mia. Hearing her story, seeing her as a person who "functions" gave me hope. Connecting with others who are "like us" brought a sense of healing, because it's a place to talk about our precious babies with others who understand this tremendous sense of pain. If you feel you are unable to meet face-to-face, there are also online support meetings or companions who have lost children that can email you and communicate with you through whatever platform is most comfortable for you.

You may have friends who are looking to support you in any way possible. Don't be afraid to tell them what you need. Even if it's nothing, just tell them you don't need anything now, but you will need them later. Having someone to call and just listen is a HUGE support. The supportive friend doesn't have to have the answers, it's just a way for the grieving parent to let go of feelings and emotions that are eating at them. If you are supporting a grieving friend, you may need to be the one to initiate and continue contact. Be sure to call and check in if you haven't heard from your grieving friend in a while.

CHAPTER 4

Significant Days

There will be days ahead on your journey that seem easy and then - BAM! - something hits you like a bus and that specific trigger that will set you back to ground zero. When that happens, know that you are not alone. Again, try to find that one person who will be your sounding board. Family, friends, someone from a support group, or a journal, getting your feelings out will help you on hard days during this journey.

You may also know of days that are coming ahead that hold significance. You can try to prepare for those days by planning ahead for something fun. A friend of mine plans a special family day every year on her son's birthday. It's a way to be together as a family, honor their sweet baby and support each other.

If you are supporting someone in the grief journey, it's important for you to keep track of significant days. As a grieving parent, we can feel like others have forgotten our babies. One of the hardest days was about a month after Mia passed and I went to the mailbox and there wasn't a sympathy card to open. The next day either. Then it hit me, others have moved on, but I haven't. Then my sister-in-law called me on the one month anniversary of Mia's passing to check on me. That was huge. She didn't forget Mia. I have had other friends and family members send cards on her birthday which is always heartwarming. Mia always has an Easter basket each year. It's little things like this that go a long way in our healing.

As a caregiver for friends or family, set a reminder to give them a call, send a card or give a gentle reminder that you still remember, especially on significant days or anniversaries. Grieving parents want their babies lives to never be forgotten.

CHAPTER 5

Returning to Work

Going back to work after having a baby is hard. But, going back to work after having a baby who has passed away can be extremely difficult. Returning to work means facing reality and beginning life with a new normal. You are no longer able to hide behind the walls of comfort. You are forced to face people. There may be "looks." There are questions. Most return to work as a way to forget about the grief for a while and focus on the job at hand, but with the uncertainty of how it all will go, it can make one uneasy. One way to handle this, is to talk to your boss or a trusted co-worker prior to your return. Let them know your wishes. Some may want to talk about their baby, because it's our way to "share" them with others. So, it wouldn't bother you if others ask questions. However, some may not want to stir up emotions, so you'd prefer for it to be "business as usual." Your boss or co-worker can convey how you'd like for things to be handled when you come back. You can decide what you want your colleagues to know in your own time. It may be best to start with half days if you are able and transition into full days. As a teacher, I went back but was allowed to have the sub in the room with me the first week so I could ease into the transition back.

CHAPTER 6

Sharing With Others

One of the first times I went to the store with Eric after Mia passed away the cashier looked at Eric sitting in the cart commenting on how cute he was. Then she asked a question... "How many kids do you have?" I froze. I didn't know what to say. 'Two... I have two kids!' I screamed in my head. But, how do I explain to this stranger what I've been through? That I have two, but one died. So I told her, " I have just the one." I got into the car and cried the whole way home. I felt such guilt. How could I have said that? How could I have dismissed the importance of Mia's life? The next time that question was asked, I answered honestly and I got an uncomfortable pause and a "you poor thing," which made me wish I had lied. If it's one thing I've learned over the years about this question -"How many kids do you have?" - it's that you'll learn who you answer truthfully to and who you don't. I figured out that I don't need to share my life's story with the cashier and deal with awkward interactions. Instead, when the time and place arises with those I am closer to, I can share Mia with them. I don't have to feel guilty for not including Mia in certain answers. It's just easier for me (and for them) if I don't. So, if you are asked this question, feel free to answer how you see fit during that time and don't feel guilty. It doesn't mean you have forgotten your baby or that they are not important. It simply makes things easier for you in your journey to healing.

When I lost Mia in 2001, social media was nonexistent. There wasn't a platform to share feelings, experiences or connect with others. This topic of pregnancy and infant loss was still a bit taboo. As I finally found my way to Facebook in 2009, it was then that I was able to share a little about Mia with many who didn't know about my loss. Sharing a picture of her on her birthday with a message of love, opened the doors for others to tell me about their own loss. In my opinion, social media can be a good thing and it can be a bad thing. It's bad for us in a way that we often see a "highlight" reel of our friends lives and can get caught up in the comparison game. We can get consumed with our time and disconnect from what is happening around us. However, social media has been proven positive as it has allowed for real connections to be made, especially in the healing journey. I was surprised at how many friends wanted to know more about Mia's story and I was ready to tell! Eight years after her loss, I was ready to share more of her with others. As social media has grown, there are groups and platforms that have formed to allow others to share their loss, experience and be real and authentic with one another. A topic that was once forbidden, is now very front and center. To the point that celebrities are taking to social media to share open and honestly about their own struggles with pregnancy and infant loss. When we hear others share, it's a way for us to say, "Me too!" The more we can talk about our babies, share our stories, (their story) we can work on our healing and help others in the process.

CHAPTER 7

Sibling Grief

When I lost Mia, Eric was only 18 months, so I didn't think he truly understood what was going on. I was so wrong. I should've known. After all, he'd kiss my belly all the time. We had been preparing him for a little sister that would be in the room next door. Eric didn't get to meet Mia until after she died. He kissed her and hugged her. But, after she died, I wasn't so focused on his feelings. One - I was just trying to get through each day as best I could. Two - I didn't think he'd understand the concept of death. However, as he grew, and we talked about her, and he'd look at her pictures that were displayed, he began to ask questions. I tried to answer as honest and as simply as I could.

We participated in a memory walk for several years after Mia passed. When Eric was about four we picked up our shirts for the walk. I remember we got in the car and he just started crying. "What's wrong, buddy?" I asked. He said, "I miss Mia." He saw her pictures all the time. We'd talk about her as a family and I realized, he was grieving too. I didn't think about his feelings along the way. So, from then on, I worked on ways that he could express what he was feeling. I let him draw, share and tell me more. He helped make her birthday cakes. Once when we were on vacation in Mexico, he was drinking a slushee and looking up at the sky. He said, "Mom, I bet Mia is having a Bahama Mama too." I loved his heart and that he was always thinking about her.

When he started school, I had to tell the teachers that he might say he has two sisters, and he's telling the truth. Through the years, he brought home art work and essays about his sister. On her 16th birthday, he suggested we all get dressed up and go to dinner to celebrate her birthday. Eric happened to get sick and when we mentioned the idea to postpone the dinner, he made it clear that the dinner would go on. One of the most touching parts of that day was before we left for dinner, Tony and I went to visit Mia's grave site. As we were about to leave, a car pulled up. Out of the car came Molly and a friend. Molly had flowers in her hand to place on Mia's grave. As Tony and I drove home together, we realized how Mia has impacted her siblings lives.

During Eric's senior year of high school, he got his first tattoo. I'd allow it as long as it had meaning. His tattoo was an arrow with a compass in the middle pointing up to God to show that God will always lead him. In the middle of his compass was an "M" for Mia. (How could I say no to that?) When his friends saw the tattoo, they asked what the "M" was for. My sister, was his only response. Since most knew of his sister, Molly that was a strange thought for them. I love that he didn't feel the need to explain anything to them. Which serves as a great reminder for all of us. We don't always need to explain everything to everybody.

Our daughter Molly, is our rainbow baby. As she has grown, all she knows are the stories we tell. When she was little she'd tag along to candlelight vigils and walks, help make her birthday cakes or partake in whatever else we did to honor Mia. As she grew older, I'd always give her the option of participating. I never wanted her to feel like she had to. But she never missed. When asked how she felt about Mia, Molly shared with me that she's never felt forced to attend her events, but that it was just something she should do because she's here and Mia isn't. In her mind, Mia died so that she could live, and she truly believes that she is meant to be here as a part of God's

plan. (We had shared that we had only planned to have two kids). So, she senses her life has a greater purpose and with that, she places high expectations on herself because she needs to live up to a high standard. She assures me I never put the pressure on her, it's just how she views life. Molly often wonders what Mia would've been like. Would they have been the same or complete opposites? She lets her mind wander and think about what life would be like if she, Eric and Mia were all here. When she says that, I realize, I've never had that thought. I too often wonder about what Mia would look like, if she'd be the same as or different from Molly, but I never thought about having all three of my kids together. Molly says she's here to do something big, something good. She too, wants a tattoo to honor Mia and to remind her of that message. "For the good" along with Mia's date of birth and date of death, is what she plans to have inked on her someday. I love that both of the kids can give such different perspectives on this event that changed the course of our family. I love that Mia still can be a big part of this family all these years later.

Of course all kids will handle grief differently. I think that it's most important to be honest and upfront with your children about what has happened. Encourage your children to share their feelings and provide various outlets for them to do so. For Molly especially, I never wanted her to feel like a replacement. Including your baby into family conversations and events can help keep their memory alive.

CHAPTER 8

Holiday Grief

Holidays for most are a time of celebration and remembrances. For those who are grieving, it's a reminder of who isn't sitting at the table this year. Since Mia was born in December, it has made Christmas more difficult for us. I'll never forget standing in line to visit Santa with Eric. I would look at all the babies in strollers. I even felt guilty for looking at a teenage mom and wondering why she was able to have a healthy baby and I wasn't. Shame on me for thinking that, but grief can stir up a lot of negative emotions. We tried hard to make Christmas special for Eric, but it was so hard to smile. There was guilt. How could I smile? How could I celebrate? I just lost my baby. The day after Christmas I remember literally chucking the nearly needless tree out the front door. I was done with that holiday. To this day, my husband Tony has a very difficult time with Christmas as it stirs up a lot of emotions and pain.

The following year, while we were still grieving, we were also planning for another baby. While we were focusing on a new baby, we also wanted to honor Mia. We wanted to plan something special for her birthday. I learned through the Share organization of a candlelight vigil that is held every year on December 6th at The Angel of Hope. If you don't know the story behind the Angel of Hope, it originated in a fictional book, The Christmas Box by Richard Paul Evans. This book has helped to place hundreds of statues around the world. It was a blessing that there was a statue just minutes from my home. This was a perfect way to celebrate her December 4th birthday. Since I never had the opportunity to make birth announcements, I used the only picture I have of her with her eyes open to create a beautiful invitation for family and close friends to come to the house for cake. Afterwards we all caravanned to the nearby park and gathered to remember Mia and other babies gone too soon. Each year we have continued to gather in rain, sleet, snow, and freezing temps to hear songs, poems and an uplifting message that brings hope to grieving families during the holiday season. For our family, it's Mia's birthday celebration.

The Share organization along with local funeral homes and hospitals plan special evenings during December to support those who are grieving during the holiday season. It's a special time to come together with others who feel that emptiness and it can open a door to connect with others or just feel a sense of peace to know you're not alone during this season.

CHAPTER 9

Father's Grief

Grief looks different on everyone. Especially between men and women. My husband, Tony, was there when it all happened. He watched Mia pass away. Almost 18 years later, he can still tell me every detail of what happened before I got to the hospital. The memory that will never leave my mind is the elevator doors opening to the Labor and Delivery floor and Tony standing right there when they opened. As soon as he saw me he burst into tears and I knew. I fell into him and he pulled me up. He held me up for quite a long time. In his opinion, it was his job to be strong for me, because that's what men are "supposed to do." He decided to return to work right away. He felt a routine would be good for him. However, that didn't leave a lot of time for him to truly process what happened and understand his feelings and emotions around it all. We had attended a support group for a few months after Mia passed away. He did like that he wasn't the only man there. However, we didn't stay with the group for very long because I became pregnant with Molly shortly after. We didn't want to upset others who were struggling to have one baby be reminded of

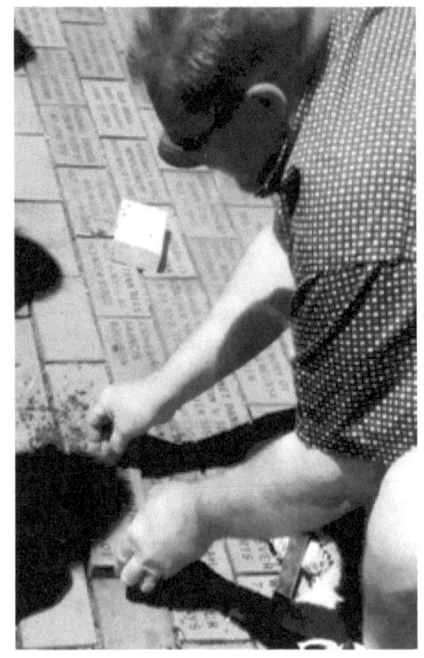

that pain with my growing belly. So because of that, he never got to form a deep connection with these other men to confide in. It seemed that all who were close to him thought if you don't talk about it, all will be ok. He needed someone to take him out, to let him vent. If you are supporting a grieving father, check on them too. It's just as important for them to deal with the emotions of grief and to also feel supported.

Tony struggled with how to be a Dad to Mia too. Friends of ours had gifted to us a memorial brick to be placed around the Angel of Hope statue. The first spring after Mia passed, there was a brick laying ceremony to allow parents to place the bricks. For Tony, this was very healing. He felt for the first time he was doing something for Mia. He dug away the dirt, placed it and set it there permanently. Each time we return he touches it. It's a gentle reminder of something he was able to do for her.

As we have talked, Tony has shared that part of his grieving is because he didn't really know Mia. I was able to have her grow inside me and feel her move. Sure, he put his hand on my belly and would talk to her, but there was still a disconnect from knowing her the way I knew her. When we visit her gravesite, for many years we always went separately. This was Tony's way of having his own time with her. I could see how important that was for him. I'd let him buy his own flowers or trinkets to place on her grave. This was another way he could do something "for her."

For many years, Tony never fully slept through the night. He often replayed the night of Mia's passing in his head. He allowed himself to get caught up in the "what if" game too. As we have shared within our small group at church, he's found a place where he can talk a little more freely about his feelings about Mia. I wish he had had more opportunities early on to talk. Grieving fathers often don't get the attention and support that they truly need.

CHAPTER 10
Mother's Grief

As a mother, from the time we find out we are carrying a baby inside of us, something changes. It's hard to put into words how you can love someone so incredibly much even before meeting them. Maybe this is why the grief seems so much harder. We want others to know our babies. We want to talk about them, but how?

It's taken many years for pregnancy and infant loss to become a topic of conversation. In the past, society made it unacceptable to discuss infancy loss. I knew that my grandmother had lost a child at birth from my mom, but never from my grandmother herself. She was there when Mia passed away. Still, she never shared about her own experience, even when I asked. I am so grateful we are in a time where we don't have to bury our feelings.

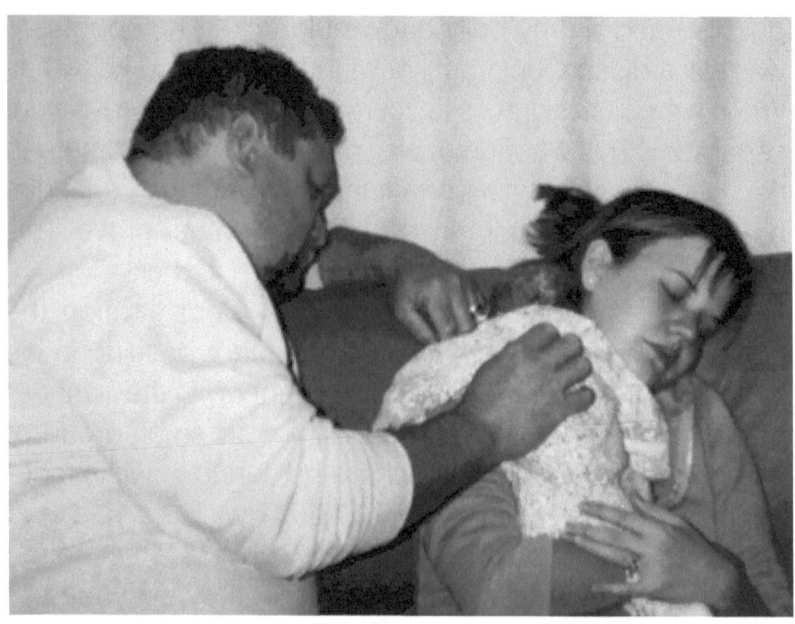

Before returning to work, I spent a lot of time creating a memory book for Mia. This was a great outlet for me to focus on while I had the time. I participated in walks in Mia's name and volunteered for a few events through Share along the way. However for me, a huge part of my grief turned into anxiety. Having all three of my children so sick, so young and losing one, can do a number on you. I've been to counselors and therapists along the way. And nearly 18 years later, I finally placed the word trauma on my pain. I've been through a traumatic event and it's changed me. My turning point was the school shooting at Sandy Hook Elementary in 2012. The shooting took place in December, 11 years and 5 days after Mia passed. On my drive to work the morning after the shooting, hearing the news reports hit me. I literally bawled to the point I had a panic attack. I had to call my friend to talk me off the ledge. For me that shooting drug up my past pain of losing Mia. As an elementary teacher, my heart broke for those parents who were sending their child off to school never to see them again. But my anxiety over the years was the fear of losing my children. This shooting was my fear coming true in a way. That I could lose my other children, now in a more horrific way.

The news that week made me a total mess. I had spotted bruises on Molly's arms and legs. She didn't complain about them. She plays soccer, so most likely from that. However, I literally let my mind think she had some rare cancer. I couldn't let it go. Tony told me to make an appointment with the doctor to gain a sense of peace. Our general practitioner knew our story and understood my irrational thoughts and helped to put me at ease that she's an active 10 year old, but drew her blood anyway to reassure me. I felt like a crazy person. Seriously, who puts their child through that?

It was then that I began to notice my relationship with God(or lack of one). I had gone to church my whole life. I was confirmed, I took my kids to Sunday school faithfully. I was active in the church. I was doing everything I was "supposed" to do. I had noticed that my son, Eric had a deep faith in God. He would often share stories of what he learned in Sunday School and Confirmation class. He would ask me questions that I couldn't answer. I was embarrassed that my son knew more about the bible than I did. This was when I began to tap into know God on a more personal level. I discovered the verse, Psalm 37:4, "Delight yourself in the Lord, and he will give you the desires of your heart." My desire was to walk without fear. To live life how I was supposed to live, how Mia would want me to live. I was able to meet women that mentored me and helped to grow my relationship with God. I found a new church home that welcomed our family with open arms and loved us right where we were. I've completed several bible studies, including one with Molly that focused on fear. I've learned that whenever fear creeps in, that I can follow Philippians 4:8 "Fix your eyes on what is true, and honorable, and right and pure and lovely and admirable. Think about such things that are excellent and praiseworthy." I realized I was focused on everything in my life that has gone wrong or could go wrong, rather than thinking about what is praiseworthy. I need to focus on the good. I had fallen back into the bitterness trap rather than living better. A gratitude journal helped me focus on the better parts each day. Tony and I ended up in a couples small group at church that allowed us to form some of the strongest relationships with friends. It's been a safe place to open up about our struggles with Mia, even all these years later. I shared with them a dream of mine was to write a book about Mia and they've been nothing but encouraging since I spoke that dream. They are the reason you are reading this.

CHAPTER 11

Honor Their Memories

Grief isn't an easy process. As you can see, there are steps forward and backward, but just keep taking the steps to move forward. Even if you tiptoe, you'll be moving in the right direction. Just know that you can and will get through this. Most importantly, know that your grief journey is your own. It is a process that you will have to walk through. There's no time frame either. I've been on this journey for 18 years and still walk it each day. If you are new to this grief or have been walking it for a while, honoring your baby is a wonderful way to heal. There have been many things that I have done over the years to help me honor Mia's memory.

Part of your journey will be to find a way to honor your baby's memory. Memories are what exist after a loved one dies, we can hold onto what we've created with that special person. However, for our precious babies, I think this is what we grieve the most. 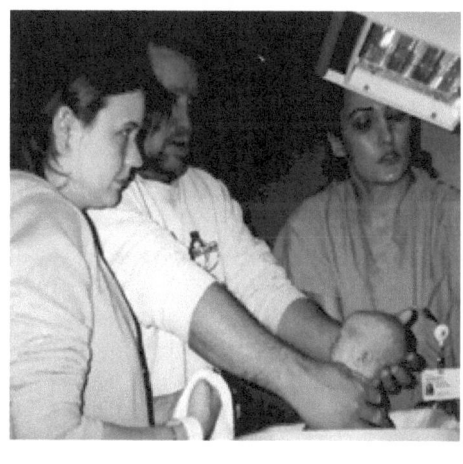 We are robbed of the opportunity to create memories and experiences together with our child. So how can we find ways to hold onto this sweet life that was taken much too soon? Keepsakes can bring a sense of comfort and provide a small way to hold onto the children we have lost. We can show our love and honor their life in our own special ways, such as memory walks, making their birthday cakes, we imagine their life in Heaven, we create missions and charities, in this way, it becomes another way we share them with family and friends. It is also helpful in the journey to healing.

CHAPTER 12

Pictures are Priceless

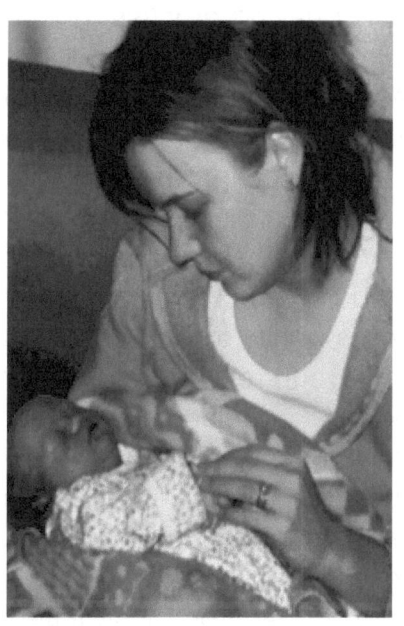

Although it's been 18 years, I can recall almost every detail of my baby, Mia, after she suddenly passed away. What helps me to recall those details are the pictures that were taken shortly afterwards. A nurse came in and brought a small disposable camera for us to take pictures, but I let the camera sit. Finally, my sister-in-law, a NICU nurse, picked up the camera and started taking pictures. I remember her saying, "you'll want these later." Was she ever right. These pictures have become my most prized possessions. They are a part of Mia's story. With the photography today, there are so many beautiful ways to capture your baby and family together. You may not want to view the pictures right away, but you will be ready for them some day. A framed picture on display is a forever reminder of how your baby is a part of your family. For us, it shows our other children that she's a part of our family too. Hospitals have resources to help you find a photographer if you are not able. The hospital will assist with collecting handprints, footprints, locks of hair, and swaddling blankets. Don't be afraid to ask. All these things help tell your baby's story.

CHAPTER 13

Journal the Journey

At some point when you're ready, sit down and write a record of your baby's birth story. First of all, it is actually a very healing outlet during the grieving process. (I journaled mine just three days after. Looking back on it, I'm glad I did because there were details I had written that I had forgotten.) You can then take your story and pair it with the pictures, prints, certificates and other mementos and create a scrapbook. This is a place to hold your baby's story and share it easily with friends or family. This was perfect for when I returned to work. I left it out in the lounge and others had the opportunity to get to "know" Mia through my eyes. I didn't have to retell my story over and over. Digital scrapbooks are popular and another way to easily compose a book of your baby's life. In my scrapbook, my husband and I each wrote a letter to Mia about our thoughts and feelings as a way to help us walk through our grief journey. These letters were written shortly after she passed away. Looking back on these letters now, I am able to see how far we've come from that pain. I've included those letters for you to see.

Mia Suzanne Linck,

I just don't know where to begin with this letter. The impact you have made on me, your mother, brother and the rest of your family. I have put this letter off for about two weeks because I don't know what all I want to say. To begin, I want you to know I think of you every day, all day long. Your mother and I are so proud of how hard you fought in the hospital. To tell you that I love you is an understatement. My life will never be the same without you. All the days I spent crying I don't know if it was how sad I was to lose you or because of how much it hurt knowing I can never hold you in my arms again. I am going to miss you growing up and all the father-daughter events we were supposed to do together. I want you to know your spirit will never be forgotten. Your pictures will always be displayed and we will tell everyone we know about our beautiful daughter Mia Suzanne Linck. I can't explain how bad I feel when we load up the car to go somewhere and you're not with us. I want to cry every time but I know I need to be strong for mom and Eric. Holidays are really hard right now but knowing you're with us when we light "Mia's" candles helps out. I could never explain how much I love you, but I hope you realize how much I do. Needless to say, I will never forget you, stop missing you, loving you or calling you my daughter and second child.

I LOVE YOU MIA,

Dad

Dear Mia,

This is the hardest letter I've ever had to write. I thought I would have a lifetime to tell you everything I have to say. It hurts so much knowing that you're gone and I've lost the opportunity to teach you so many things. Life is so unfair. I did everything right for you and it hurts to know that other Mommies have their healthy babies when maybe they weren't as caring to their bodies as me. I had so many dreams for you Mia, and it's hard knowing they'll never come true. I will see a little girl with blonde hair and wonder if that's what you would have looked like. But then I remember what a beautiful girl you were and remember the delicate features you had and know that girl doesn't even compare to you. As much as I dream about it, I know I can't go back and change what has happened. I have to accept what has happened and like your Daddy has said, find the positives out of this whole experience. The biggest positive was you. If someone told me when I was pregnant that I would only have 5 days, I still would have had you. Feeling you grow and move inside me was such a gift. You were teaching me about your personality and about one of life's hardest lessons. I believe with all my heart that your gift to your Daddy and me was your strength. From the womb to your entrance into this world your strength was shown. I am so proud of you and touched by your presence. You fought hard to stay with us for as long as you could. With all the reports back now, I know the infection was hurting far more than you were showing. And even if by some miracle you were able to be with us today, the quality of life you would've had would not be the life we would have chosen for you. God has a plan for all of us and his plan for you is special. I feel that we will continue to learn more about God's plan for you as we continue to heal. But for now, I know that part of your plan was the gift of strength. If this is your gift to us, I plan to take it and use it to the best of my ability. I tell people that it's hard not being able to show you off or brag about what new thing you're able to do, but I can show off your strength through me. Thank you so much my sweet baby girl for your life and touching so many hearts. I only hope that your dad and I touched your heart half as much as you did ours. You're in my heart forever and always.

I LOVE YOU,

Mommy

CHAPTER 14
A Chest Full of Hope

You will find that many family and friends want to support you while you grieve. You may acquire plethora of angels, books and other small items to remember your baby. While all these things are meaningful and help provide healing, it can be overwhelming to display them. A hope chest or a small box is a lovely way to preserve any keepsakes from your child's life, including outfits, blankets, and even sympathy cards. I cherish the hope chest that my brother made for us, and from time to time I will go through the treasures I've placed in my daughter's chest.

CHAPTER 15

Charms that bring Comfort

Most women wear jewelry, so why not wear something to remind you of your baby on a daily basis? It can be something you touch as you find yourself thinking about your child to help ease your mind. Often times, bereaved parents can find it difficult that they don't have opportunities to talk about their child. A piece of jewelry with your baby's date or name can perhaps become a conversation starter that will allow you to share your baby with others if you choose. Jewelry isn't just for women either. Grieving dads can also wear pieces specific to their child. I gave my husband a necklace with a small angel charm for Christmas after we lost Mia. Tony will often feel the necklace when he thinks of her. He never takes it off as it's his reminder that she is always with him.

CHAPTER 16
Family Creations

When I knew our family was complete, I started a tradition of a family "Birthday Plate", a way to have our favorite meal as we celebrate our birthdays. Our family went to one of those places where you paint your own pottery. We painted our hands and placed our handprint and birthdates on the plate. In order to incorporate Mia on our plate, I took her handprint and outlined it on clear transparency paper and cut it out as a stencil with an Exacto knife. Each year, we make a special cake or treat for Mia's birthday. There are countless other ways you can create unique keepsakes for you or your family as the years go on. Framed pictures, casts and ornaments are some popular ideas. It's never too late to design something in your baby's honor.

CHAPTER 17

Foundations & Fundraisers

Beside physical mementos, there are also other ways to honor your baby's memory. Many families choose to create a foundation or will participate in a charity event in their child's name. The physical act of "doing something" is a way to feel like you are parenting your child. Working a charitable event also allows for friends and family to become involved and provide continued support after the loss of the baby. My friend Emily created "Parker's Army" after her son, Parker Ray passed away from complications of Charge Syndrome. Parker's Army has helped with many events in the community, including an annual blood drive as a way to give back since Parker needed blood transfusions himself. Each year in October, Share holds a "Walk to Remember." Many families gather in matching t-shirts to honor their babies. It's a great fundraiser to raise awareness and support for those families who are grieving. There are so many great causes to help in memory of a loved one.

CHAPTER 18

Grow a Garden

You may choose to plant a tree or place a statuary in the yard or garden. We planted a pink dogwood in the spring after Mia's passing. We've watched it grow as she would've here on Earth, and each year when it blooms, we think of her.

There are so many special ways to honor our precious babies. Keepsakes and memory making serve as reminders that our babies lives mattered and were so important to us. Whatever you choose, it will come from a place of love and will be a way to provide a sense of comfort for you and your family.

Conclusion

Too many of us have been written one of the most difficult stories to read. However, no matter where you are in your journey, you are not alone. One way to honor our babies is to continue to take the step each day to live our best life, because it's how we lead our lives that will help tell our baby's story. I pray that you find yourself living better instead of bitter each day as you move forward. Keep focus on all the positive ways your baby has impacted your life (and how they will continue to do so) and I hope you will find peace and comfort in the days and years ahead.

Made in United States
Troutdale, OR
08/26/2025